More About Retrogrades

Helen Adams Garrett

ISBN-10: 0-86690-532-4
ISBN-13: 978-0-86690-532-9

First Printing: 1991
Current Printing: 2011

Cover Deisgn: Jack Cipolla

Published by:
American Federation of Astrologers, Inc.
6535 S. Rural Road
Tempe AZ 85283

www.astrologers.com

Printed in the United States of America

Contents

What Are Retrogrades   1

Interpreting Retrograde Planets   9

Health and Retrograde Planets   55

Progressed and Transiting Retrograde Planets   69

What Are Retrogrades?

There are two systems of logging the placement of planets: heliocentric and geocentric. Heliocentric viewing originates as if from the Sun and geocentric has its point of origin from Earth.

Heliocentric positions are never retrograde because the view is as if from the Sun, watching the astral bodies travel around the Sun. The view from Earth (geocentric) is like watching the planets from one of them.

Now put yourself in an automobile and cast your eyes toward another vehicle as it moves alongside you. No doubt at some time you have been in a parked car when one next to you started to move and you hit your brake because it felt as though your car was drifting away. That equates to the sensation from Earth as we rotate around the Sun in relationship to the other planets. This then is what we refer to as retrograde. Literally it means to move backward.

Terms of Retrograde
- *Mercury:* Approximately every fourth month, usually three times per year, for a period of twenty to twenty-four days.

- *Venus:* Approximately 580 days for a period of about forty days.
- *Mars:* A little more than two years for a period of fifty-six to eighty-two days.
- *Jupiter:* Every year for a period of approximately 120 days.
- *Saturn:* Every year for a period of approximately 140 days.
- *Uranus:* Every year for a period of approximately 148 days.
- *Neptune:* Every year for a period of approximately 150 days.
- *Pluto:* Every year for a period of 150 to 155 days.
- *Moon:* Never.

Retrograde Patterns

Mercury: As an average, Mercury goes retrograde three times a year, but about every sixth year the retrograde station is made four times. Mercury also makes the direct station following each retrograde period. As a rule, the retrograde station is made in the same element all year.

Mercury, when conjunct the Sun, can be retrograde or direct. If Mercury is direct when conjunct the Sun, the next conjunction will occur when Mercury is retrograde, and vice versa.

The rule for retrograde is that the planet is nearest Earth in its transit. Since Earth is always exactly opposite the Sun by sign and degree, Mercury is conjunct Earth when retrograde. A planet appears to be in the same sign with the Sun and is so recorded. From the heliocentric view, Mercury and Earth are more in line and are conjunct at the midpoint (peak) of the retrograde period.

Venus: The pattern of Venus is not as well defined as Mercury. It occurs about nineteen months after the previous retrograde date.

Mars: Mars is retrograde at approximately two-year intervals. Its pattern is erratic, remaining retrograde from fifty-six to eighty-two days and sometimes holding the stationary degree for as long as twenty-five days. On a geocentric chart, if Mars is retrograde, it will be found on the opposite side of the chart from the Sun. From cycle to cycle, the retrograde station moves forward one whole sign plus a few degrees in the next cycle.

Jupiter: The average retrograde place is very near a trine aspect, which means that when Jupiter turns retrograde, it is very near a trine with the Sun. When the retrograde period comes to a close and Jupiter makes its direct station, it is again in a trine aspect with the Sun. A trine has Jupiter energy.

Saturn: Saturn's cycle is more regular, and heliocentric Saturn will be near the same degree as geocentric Saturn.

The average number of degrees the Sun moves while Saturn is retrograde is 135, which represents the sesquiquadrate, which means difficulty. A sesquiquadrate is a square (ninety degrees) plus a semisquare (forty-five degrees). The energy of difficulty is obstacles plus interference, implying that when Saturn is retrograde in direct aspect to a chart that these energies will be experienced during that retrograde cycle concerning issues indicated by other planet or planets, signs and houses. As you will see later, there are other minor aspects between Saturn and Sun while Saturn is retrograde.

This is a time to take stock of people who are interfering and to learn what the karma might be with those individuals.

One should also consider the act that is being interfered with as to its karmic effect.

Uranus: Uranus is retrograde every year when the Sun transits in opposition to Uranus.

The Sun is just short of an inconjunct with Uranus—148 degrees—at the retrograde and direct stations, indicating out-of-control conditions. The inconjunct energy requires service or change.

Neptune: Neptune is retrograde each year as the Sun transits in opposition to Neptune. When the word "opposition" is used in a general statement in reference to retrogrades it is to say that the planet is on the opposite side of the chart from Sun.

Neptune has a rhythmic cycle when the planet goes retrograde and then direct two or three degrees, advances four to six degrees and back two or three, then forward four to six again. This pattern repeats year after year. The Sun moves approximately 155 degrees as this planetary rotation is in process.

Pluto: When Pluto was transiting Taurus, it lingered there thirty-two years, and the Sun moved up to 170 degrees each year during the retrograde period. In the late 1990s, Pluto rushed through Scorpio, completing its tour of that sign in fewer than twelve years.

Once the positions of the planets have changed, it requires about 25,000 years before they will be back in the exact same alignment. During that period of time, untold numbers of configurations occur. That is to say, it is that long before there will ever be another time when the planets are exactly the same as in your birth chart.

The Sun and Moon are not planets, nor are they ever retrograde. We cannot count Earth, even though it is a planet, because it is the relationship of other planets to Earth that constitutes a retrograde condition. Excluding Earth, there are eight other planets definitely placed and identified at this time in history. They are in order of distance from Sun: Mercury, Venus, Earth, Mars, Jupiter, Saturn, Uranus, Neptune, Pluto.

In researching, we find that there are times when there are no planets retrograde, but we have not found a time when all eight planets were retrograde at the same time.

John McCormick, in his *The Book of Retrogrades*, dealt primarily with the number of planets in a chart that were retrograde. He found that certain expressions of energy seem to apply to each given number of planets retrograde:

- None: Expend enormous physical effort.
- One: Works alone, achieves alone.
- Two: Depends upon public acceptance.
- Three: Determination to excel.
- Four: Seeks expression in private.
- Five: Solitary occupation.
- Six and Seven: No conclusions.

Planets from Mars outward, when retrograde, are on the opposite side of the chart from the Sun. This means you attract people who tend not to cooperate and who take advantage of you. Lack of cooperation and being taken advantage of might be karmic, and a more intricate study of that retrograde planet might be enlightening.

Two or three planets are retrograde at one time more than fifty percent of the time. Seldom are there no planets retrograde and rarely are there seven planets retrograde.

In the past 200 years, there have been seven planets retrograde on these dates:

- January 12-31, 1884
- January 30-February 6, 1886
- May 1-4, 1984

This list of dates was compared with dates of disasters in the *World Almanac* to ascertain what kinds of events would dominate. No records were found of any disastrous events on any of the days when there were seven planets retrograde. If four or more retrogrades seem to belong to those who are aggressively defensive military generals, are we to suspect that even in events, collective retrograde energy in nature and the universe takes similar form?

Let us say that the six outer planets, considering Mars as one since it is outside Earth, plus either Mercury or Venus are retrograde. This means that if Sun were to be placed on the Ascendant of an equal house chart that all six of the outer planets would be on the western half of the chart. One would instantly conclude that the individual is subject to the action of others. The planets might be in close proximity or stellium, or they might be scattered from the fifth house through the ninth. This means that the person is almost completely dependant upon or subject to others or must submit to combat or service. If this is karma, what better way to spend a lifetime than defending a better cause? John McCormick said that military generals often have four or five planets retrograde.

Since retrogrades are believed to connect with karmic episodes, perhaps it behooves us to be more careful to cultivate our karmic obligations into debts paid rather than adopting a "get even" attitude, which could establish more undesirable records for future lifetimes. Nice things happen with retro-grades, more than once!

Interpreting
Retrograde Planets

A planet retrograde has a different energy, just as the direct rays of the Sun are not the same as those that are reflected from a solid surface. Always take into consideration the fact that it is a planet's relationship to Earth and Sun that creates a retrograde condition.

Earth, if logged on your chart, would be at the exact degree and minute opposite the Sun on the chart. Planets are always near Earth when retrograde. Mercury and Venus will appear in your tropical Placidus chart very near the Sun because geocentric viewing of the planets never allows Mercury to be more than twenty-eight degrees from the Sun, and Venus is never more than forty-eight degrees from the Sun. If Mercury is retrograde and a heliocentric chart was drawn, you would find it in a sign on the other side of the chart.

Some examples are:

Mercury Geo	Mercury Helio	Sun	Earth
29 Aries Rx	16 Virgo	14 Aries	14 Libra
27 Aries Rx	7 Libra	19 Aries	19 Libra
24 Aries Rx	24 Libra	24 Aries	24 Libra

20 Aries Rx	10 Scorpio	29 Aries	29 Libra
18 Aries Rx	25 Scorpio	4 Taurus	4 Scorpio
16 Aries D	6 Sagittarius	8 Taurus	8 Scorpio

Note the alignment of Mercury, Sun and Earth on the third day above.

Mercury Retrograde in the Signs

For an accurate interpretation of Mercury retrograde it is important that helio Mercury be taken into consideration. To emphasize the importance of learning the helio Mercury of any particular chart, the following example is offered:

April 6, 1926, 5:00 p.m. EST, Mercury was retrograde at 4 Aries 44. On the same date, time and place, Mercury was at 2 Scorpio 23, heliocentrically. On March 10, 1999, 5:00 p.m. EST, Mercury was retrograde at 4 Aries 03, within minutes of the April 6, 1926 placement, but helio Mercury was at 17 Leo 15 in 1999.

The difference is that in 1926, Mercury was one week from going direct, and in 1999, it was on the retrograde station just beginning the retrograde cycle.

What difference does it make? In 1926 Mercury in Aries blended with Scorpio, meaning intensity, resourcefulness and privacy plus mental alertness, ambition and daring to pioneer in the pursuit of knowledge. In 1999, Mercury in Aries blended with Leo, meaning leadership, ego development and mental prowess, which was added to mental alertness, ambition and daring to pioneer in the pursuit of knowledge.

Other examples of Mercury retrograde:

Geocentric   *Heliocentric*
25 Virgo 29   10 Aries 49

25 Virgo 19	24 Aquarius 19
25 Virgo 46	25 Taurus 13

What are these differences? All three have Mercury retrograde in Virgo, requiring much detail, or in the negative form, neglecting detail, working toward correcting something whether it is using personal energy or being a supervisor directing another. When coupled with Aries, it is very personal, working in detail again and again until it is right. When coupled with Aquarius, perfection is attained at personal convenience, maintaining individuality. When coupled with Taurus, perfection is attained for a price.

From these examples it can be seen that it is necessary to consult a heliocentric ephemeris in order to know the placement in relationship to geocentric Mercury.

You should also find your heliocentric Mercury even if it is direct in motion. This same manner of interpretation can be applied. As an example, my natal Cancer Mercury is direct and helio Mercury is in Taurus. The Cancer Mercury has to remember to close and rest a menu in a restaurant in order for the server to know I am ready to order; then I ask to keep the menu to read. My Taurus Mercury gets the best and most for the money. Many people over the years have expressed a desire to follow me grocery shopping because of my ability to know (Mercury) quality (Taurus) food (Cancer). I am extremely frugal, but not with family. Taurus stakes a claim on those who accept Cancer's nurturing. My students are my children (Cancer), but they pay (Taurus).

Mercury Rx in Aries

Helio Mercury will be in Leo, Virgo, Libra, Scorpio or Sagittarius. Use any standard interpretation for Mercury in

Aries, then blend.

Helio Leo: Seeks knowledge to elevate leadership, to develop ego, to build an empire, be it large or small.

Helio Virgo: Wants to be right. Seeks knowledge to improve the universe or surroundings. Prone to self improvement.

Helio Libra: Shares knowledge, self, pleasure, but likes being alone with that special someone.

Helio Scorpio: Makes own moral codes; that is, "if its right for me, its right." Proves self-worth through getting to the bottom of issues.

Helio Sagittarius: Adventurous and athletic. High physical and mental energy. Depending upon Mars, could be more a sports spectator than participant.

Mercury Rx in Taurus

Helio Mercury will be in Virgo, Libra, Scorpio, Sagittarius or Capricorn. Use any standard interpretation for Mercury in Taurus, then blend.

Helio Virgo: Seeks correct information to use in finances. Interested in growing things. The money counter.

Helio Libra: Likes a partner or consultant in money matters. Extremely polite or fights a fair but hard battle.

Helio Scorpio: Determined to succeed but does not boast. Learns slowly but completely and does not forget an injustice.

Helio Sagittarius: Great instinct for knowing consumer responses. Travels for pleasure and often gets paid for it.

Helio Capricorn: Terrific for business. Does not waste time. Makes use of communication. Ability in investing.

Mercury Rx in Gemini

Helio Mercury will be in Libra, Scorpio, Sagittarius, Capricorn or Aquarius. Use a standard interpretation for Mercury in Gemini, then blend.

Helio Libra: Truly the social butterfly, being loving, polite, interesting and keeping tab on everybody's latest phone number and address. Probably witty.

Helio Scorpio: Could be outstanding private detective or most vicious gossip' due to the ability to know the untold and has knowledge in general directions. The researcher/teacher.

Helio Sagittarius: The total knowledge gleaner with a desire to know all things great and small basic and advanced, could be the perpetual student. Inclined toward legal or philosophical knowledge.

Helio Capricorn: Gathers knowledge relating to business or possibly history, things of the past, or antiques.

Helio Aquarius: Creature of the unique. Has a curiosity for knowledge of rare sorts. Friendly and communal by nature.

Mercury Rx in Cancer

Helio Mercury will be in Scorpio, Sagittarius, Capricorn, Aquarius or Pisces. Use any standard interpretation for Mercury in Cancer, then blend.

Helio Scorpio: A true soul-searcher, deeply emotional, having interest in transformative issues both of spiritual and physical conditions.

Helio Sagittarius: Hands (Mercury) that are nurturing (Cancer) and healing (faith to restore and make well). Writer of emotional, family or historical issues.

Helio Capricorn: Living in the past but learning from former experiences. Very likely to have business in the home or work with or for family.

Helio Aquarius: Friends are family-like associates and relatives are friends. Organizations act as substitute family.

Helio Pisces: Deeply sympathetic, especially toward the unfortunate loner. Very psychic and caring. Interested in healing and spiritual wellness.

Mercury Rx in Leo

Helio Mercury will be in Sagittarius, Capricorn, Aquarius, Pisces or Aries. Use any standard interpretation for Mercury in Leo, then blend.

Helio Sagittarius: Exerts energy in ambition with a confidence that makes things happen. Very successful or can be overbearing. Lucky.

Helio Capricorn: Hard worker who benefits from past experience. Honors heritage. Ability in corporate leadership.

Helio Aquarius: Seeks partner who is best friend. Possessive, but demands personal freedom. May suddenly change job or career later in life.

Hello Pisces: Indulges in personal pleasures but definitely can be the life of the party, an entertainer. Excellent dancer.

Helio Aries: Royalty plus! Encourages children to be athletic and studious. Is the king or queen of the household in communications.

Mercury Rx in Virgo

Helio Mercury will be in Capricorn, Aquarius, Pisces, Aries or Taurus. Use any standard interpretation for Mercury in Virgo, then blend.

Helio Capricorn: Workaholic. Clean, clean, clean or orderly in moat areas to say the least. Probably works in something of the earth, metals, agriculture, etc.

Helio Aquarius: Emphasis on unusual health-related subjects. Creative in ways to improve sanitation, organization and environment.

Helio Pisces: Deals with health. May be a healer of the body or soul. The soul healer would be one who points out the error of the ways and offers a solution to cure fear.

Helio Aries: Majors on personal perfection through health, performance, or mental accomplishments.

Helio Taurus: Two of the food signs. Taurus rules taste buds and Virgo is food preservation. Both agriculture signs. Likely to be found in these areas or in a bank in the accounting or investment department.

Mercury Rx in Libra

Helio Mercury will be in Aquarius, Pisces, Aries, Taurus or Gemini. Use any standard interpretation for Mercury in Libra, then blend.

Helio Aquarius: Polite friendliness is the image. Creative intelligence is the code. This one steers clear of conflict.

Helio Pisces: The musician, rhythm, mental alertness, and musical feet set this one apart as beautiful. Could charm a stone or a cloud.

Helio Aries: Likes to be alone with someone in a crowd. Desires harmony but can win a war with the mind. Is quoted frequently.

Hello Taurus: Comfort is the keyword. Earns money from beauty or products of beauty or comfort. May be the spouse of a wealthy person.

Hello Gemini: Pleasure from reading. Very knowledgeable about entertainers, any subject related to interior decorating or literature.

Mercury Rx in Scorpio

Helio Mercury will be in Pisces, Aries, Taurus, Gemini or Cancer. Use any standard interpretation for Mercury in Scorpio, then blend.

Hello Pisces: Sensitive to spirit communication. Friends and relatives who have died appear frequently in image or dreams. Psychic and spiritual or totally turned off by spiritual impressions.

Helio Aries: Practices insurance in the total sense of the word. Makes effort to be insured mentally, physically and financially. Insured equals = being sure.

Helio Taurus: Is private concerning possessions and affairs of love. Devoted and passionate. Can be possessive. Does well in stock breeding.

Helio Gemini: A craving for the mysterious be it a novel, a neighborhood story, laboratory research or a harbored secret.

Helio Cancer: Dedicated to protecting home, family and homeland through secret efforts. Has many private thoughts. Holds in hurt feelings.

Mercury Rx in Sagittarius

Helio Mercury will be in Aries, Taurus, Gemini, Cancer or Leo. Use any standard interpretation for Mercury in Sagittarius, then blend.

Helio Aries: Extremely confident and outgoing. Wants own children to be athletic. Desires to be respected but hesitates to be tied down to long term obligations.

Helio Taurus: Attracted to imported materials as potential financial benefits. Hay be involved in horses or stock as income. Envoys being sports spectator.

Helio Gemini: Non-stop talker. Has knowledge on all ranges, basic to specialized. Does not like to be still. Enjoys learning. Could be perpetual student.

Helio Cancer: At home away from home. Good for writing family tree. Interest in security and protecting people.

Helio Leo: Taking pride in knowledge. Can be very dramatic. Personal successes or failures are monumental. Wants children to be accomplished.

Mercury Rx in Capricorn

Helio Mercury will be in Taurus, Gemini, Cancer, Leo or Virgo. Use any standard interpretation for Mercury in Capricorn, then blend.

Helio Taurus: Money grows from the ground, metal, trees, vegetables or fruit. Practical by nature and seeks comforts in a conservative way.

Helio Gemini: Spokesperson who deals in serious matters. Diligent in paperwork. Head of department in sales. Talks a hard bargain. Uses hands constructively.

Helio Cancer: Self controversy between business and family/home. Work may be household related, furniture, home building, etc.

Helio Leo: Takes pride in work. Gives mental abilities for executive or presidential position. Is serious concerning business.

Helio Virgo: Excessively conservative, except in potential investments. Analytical concerning business or serious issues. Capability in timing devices, clocks, regulators, etc.

Mercury Rx in Aquarius

Helio Mercury will be in Gemini, Cancer, Leo, Virgo or Libra. Use any standard interpretation for Mercury in Aquarius then blend.

Helio Gemini: Seeking unusual knowledge. Freedom of thought and speech is important. Likes to read if allowed to personally select topics.

Helio Cancer: Finds friendships within the family and treats friends like family. Is protective and nurturing toward others. Unique knowledge of foods.

Helio Leo: Is recognized as leader but has no desire to take that responsibility. A desire to be free but very careful to retain dignity. Wants personal freedom but possesses loved ones.

Helio Virgo: Has broad vocabulary, may speak in a unique way. Supports freedom for those who would otherwise be discriminated against. Self-healing ability.

Helio Libra: The social butterfly. One who is friendly without discrimination and who has charm. Knowledge may lean to things of beauty or ways of beautifying.

Mercury Rx in Pisces

Helio Mercury will be in Cancer, Leo, Virgo, Libra or Scorpio. Use any standard interpretation for Mercury in Pisces, then blend.

Helio Cancer: Will sacrifice for the family, is emotional concerning the homeland, likely candidate for the navy or other water-career. Psychic.

Helio Leo: May be a dramatic entertainer or exceptional dancer. Sensitive ego, knows what others think of him/her. Romantic. Does not see children's faults.

Helio Virgo: Self critical and willing to be self-perfecting but not always knowing what to do for self. Health conscious. Possibly photographic memory.

Helio Libra: Musical talent or interest in beauty and harmony of the environment. Sympathetic toward any seeking justice but not predecided as to justice.

Helio Scorpio: A real soul searcher and may assist others is uncovering hidden issues of the subconscious. Survives well on secret missions or in private business.

Venus Retrograde in the Signs

For better insight to Venus retrograde you want to know where heliocentric Venus was at the time of birth. It will be somewhere within the trine across the chart. Venus in Aries retrograde in the geocentric chart will find Venus heliocentrically at a degree between mid-Leo and mid-Sagittarius. As you work more with the helio placements you will come to be able in many cases to properly estimate the helio sign because the orbital rhythm of Venus is sufficiently dependable to average and estimate.

The Sun travels approximately forty-one degrees during the retrograde period, while Venus in heliocentric view travels in opposition approximately sixty-seven degrees. Example: Venus retrograded at 20 Aries on March 12, 1993 with helio Venus at 9 Virgo. Venus turned direct at 3 Aries on April 23, 1993, with helio Venus at 17 Scorpio. That is forty-one days (Sun moves forty-one degrees) and sixty-eight degrees from 9 Virgo to 17 Scorpio. You already know that when Sun is conjunct retrograde Venus that both Earth and Venus are at the exact degree opposite; add thirty-four degrees to each side of that opposition and you have your helio transit. Estimate a degree and a half per day and you are not far off.

Venus direct or retrograde rules love and money and is to be interpreted as such. The more I study astrology, the more I believe that retrogrades do not render ill. Our karma and our own .personal responses to people and issues deliver the results. Do you know anyone who collected an old debt when Venus was retrograde, bringing money back? It happens! We just remember it more when we make an unwise investment or let someone beat us in a deal.

The October 29, 1929 stock market crash is one of the most widely known financial disasters in modern history. It covered the globe in various forms, but Venus was not retrograde. The next time Venus turned retrograde was November 3, 1930 at 7 Sagittarius; it turned direct at 22 Scorpio on December 14, 1930. The significance of that is that the peak of that period was 29 Scorpio, when the Sun was conjunct Venus retrograde.

A brief interpretation of the twenty-ninth degree says "can't get enough," either because it is unavailable or because no amount can satisfy.

The opposing point from 29 Scorpio is 29 Taurus. Can't get enough money. The stock market crash was only the beginning of what followed for several years, but the most drastic financial losses were form the last week in July 1930 through 1933. Things improved only a little for about seven years, which is a Saturn cycle. On July 30, 1930, Jupiter at 6 Cancer opposed Saturn at 6 Capricorn, the business sign. Then, on September 11, 1930, Saturn made a retrograde station at 5 Capricorn, putting emphasis on the previous opposition and bringing with it a severe drought.

On June 11, 1931, Jupiter again opposed Saturn, this time at 22 Cancer-Capricorn. It rained little during the next three years. On May 1, 1930, Uranus hit a critical degree–13 Aries–and many men found a way to freedom (escape) through suicide during the next several months. Uranus in Aries represented personal freedom and the burden of depression denied that freedom.

We see from this that Venus was not the problem. Jupiter opposing Saturn coincides with business slumps, and of course the drought was a major factor in the depression of the 1930s. When crops fail, the stock market is wounded and a financial wheel changes its pace. Farmers use vehicles, transportation, chemicals and equipment, food prices escalate, consumers begin to spend less, store owners go for entertainment less, hotels have fewer guests, women cut back on cosmetics, less jewelry is sold, and on and on and on.

Interestingly, as much as Saturn was a strong element in that event, it was also Saturn's perseverance that pulled the United States up by the boot straps. Wood is ruled by Saturn, and the forestry program of cutting trees and replanting provided jobs for America. Saturn is highly evolved when it salvages instead of uses.

Venus is also love and favors and harmony and diplomacy and beauty.

Venus Rx in Aries

Helio Venus will be in Leo, Virgo, Libra, Scorpio or Sagittarius. Use any standard interpretation for Venus in Aries, then blend.

Helio Leo: I love you. I love me. I love everybody. I am romantic and dramatic. Much ambition in the financial world.

Helio Virgo: Get there first with the most and first. Prompt and organized. One lover at a time please.

Helio Libra: I love you. I want to live with you, but leave me alone for my time is MY time. I will work, but please help me.

Helio Scorpio: I told you once I love you. Do I have to tell you every time we go to the bedroom? Of course I have some secrets.

Helio Sagittarius: I want to be first to get involved in this big deal. I would rather have a weekend fling over and over even though it is with the same person than to have anyone constantly, i.e. a part-time, long-term relationship.

Venus Rx in Taurus

Helio Venus will be in Virgo, Libra, Scorpio, Sagittarius or Capricorn. Use any standard interpretation for Venus in Taurus, then blend.

Helio Venus in Virgo: Envoys gardening and counting money. Easier to love an asset than a liability, whether it be a deal or a dear.

Helio Venus in Libra: Venus rules Taurus and Libra. This one likes beauty and comfort, does not mind working but finds a comfortable way to do it. Love and leave if necessary.

Helio Venus in Scorpio: Income from private sources. Love relationships are intense and possessive. Shared possessions important in relationships.

Helio Venus in Sagittarius: Big bucks due to instinct to do the right thing at the right time. Is often separated from love by distance but adjusts to space.

Helio Venus in Capricorn: Works smart and on durable projects. Determined to make love work out.

Venus Rx in Gemini

Helio Venus will be in Libra, Scorpio, Sagittarius, Capricorn or Aquarius. Use any standard interpretation for Venus in Gemini, then blend.

Helio Venus in Libra: Very talented at sales or diplomatic communication skills and charm. Likes to go, talk and flirt. Also needs some hugs to keep personality on upswing.

Helio Venus in Scorpio: Great for research in books and papers of all kinds. Just the person to find the missing link. Can talk a long time without revealing own secrets, but not so close-mouthed otherwise.

Helio Venus in Sagittarius: Capable in export-import, jobs that do foreign trade or languages. Flirting is favorite game. Chase is better than the catch.

Helio Venus in Capricorn: Corporate executive or assistant for money. Learning the codes and investing can be profitable. Serious in love, communicative but not passionate or sensual.

Helio Venus in Aquarius: Never broke for long. Can find unusual resources and income. Friends are lovers and lovers are friends. Does not tolerate boredom.

Venus Rx in Cancer

Helio Venus will be in Scorpio, Sagittarius, Capricorn, Aquarius or Pisces. Use any standard interpretation for Venus in Cancer, then blend.

Helio Venus in Scorpio: Nurture and survive are the words here. For income insurance. Dealing in household plumbing sales or installation. Massage! Love is emotional and enduring.

Helio Venus in Sagittarius: Travel host or hostess. Parent-like counselor. Lives away from family. May marry a foreigner. Love is a ritual.

Helio Venus in Capricorn: May work in the home or be in home building business. In love relationships, vacillates between the role of parent and child.

Helio Venus in Aquarius: Does well in humane services, caring for people in an impersonal manner. Likely to fall in love with a friend. Family members are friends.

Helio Venus in Pisces: Income through sympathetic services, such as medical profession, animal care, rehabilitation or child care. Devoted in love relationships.

Venus Rx in Leo

Helio Venus will be in Sagittarius, Capricorn, Aquarius, Pisces or Aries. Use any standard interpretation for Venus in Leo, then blend.

Helio Venus in Sagittarius: Sports coach, sports pro or

athletic equipment related business. Enjoys whirlwind courtships. You'll get caught someday.

Helio Venus in Capricorn: Ambition for the satisfaction of financial success. Would hope to align with one who would be as success conscious. Loves on a practical level.

Helio Venus in Aquarius: Business or jobs come and go. Can be very career creative. Instantly in and out of love, but can settle in on a permanent relationship and like it.

Helio Venus in Pisces: Needs to be careful of easy prey for fabulous schemes. Easy money is not always sure money. A heartbreaker who gets heartbroken.

Helio Venus in Aries: Desire to own business. Does not like to work for another. Independent, but wants to know where lover is.

Venus Rx in Virgo

Helio Venus will be in Capricorn, Aquarius, Pisces, Aries or Taurus. Use any standard interpretation for Venus in Virgo, then blend.

Helio Venus in Capricorn: May be in corporate business, agriculture, cleaning or land clearing. The love relationship is not emotional but has roots and is security attached.

Helio Venus in Aquarius: Sudden changes in work or career may be experienced unless in own business, which could appropriately be electrical office equipment. May be one who wishes to remain unmarried.

Helio Venus in Pisces: Ideally employed in a field of service caring for those less fortunate or possibly in chemistry. Wants to heal the lover to a state of perfect health.

Helio Venus in Aries: Works best where there is a coordinated fast pace and where things are done right. Love of work and is primarily considerate of time and personal possessions. Right health practices may find a place.

Helio Venus in Taurus: Envoys working and being productive. Interested in ways to make more money, usually through hard work. Love nature is not mushy; rather, it is very gentle.

Venus Rx in Libra

Helio Venus will be in Aquarius, Pisces, Aries, Taurus or Gemini. Use any standard interpretation for Venus in Libra, then blend.

Helio Venus in Aquarius: Charming is the keyword, and any position which allows for polite personality without attachments is a plus. The love nature is friendly, but at certain times and under certain conditions can be affectionate.

Helio Venus in Pisces: Musician is a good guess for this talented one. Interior decorating, gifts, photography or film industry. Love nature is warm, cuddly and gentle.

Helio Venus in Aries: Enjoys legal field. Style conscious, adept in fields of clothing or wardrobe accessories. Love at first sight nature. Likes to be loved—by appointment.

Helio Venus in Taurus: Makes money in field of love, money or comfort. Knows the finer places to eat. Peaceful and harmonious, will not tolerate abuse.

Helio Venus in Gemini: Does well in any business where one needs to look good and know all. Walking encyclopedia with a pretty cover. Mental companionship is important to love relationship.

Venus Rx in Scorpio

Helio Venus will be in Places, Aries, Taurus, Gemini or Cancer. Use any standard interpretation for Venus in Scorpio, then blend.

Helio Venus in Pisces: Works well in any area requiring uncovering secrets. Also may be employed by water/sewer utility company. Love nature is private, intimate and emotional.

Helio Venus in Aries: Makes good soldier, policeman, sheriff, law enforcer, but should be in control of temperamental responses. Love nature is deeply devoted, private and sexual.

Helio Venus in Taurus: Inspector for IRS! Insurance adjuster. Mortician? Also one who transforms morals. Love nature can be possessive and may be jealous.

Helio Venus in Gemini: Could write mysteries. Crime investigator. May have interest in religion or psychic subjects. Love interest is both mental and physical.

Helio Venus in Cancer: Family control related employment, truant officer or social case worker. Love nature is emotional, intense and sensual.

Venus Rx in Sagittarius

Helio Venus will be in Aries, Taurus, Gemini, Cancer or Leo. Use any standard interpretation for Venus in Sagittarius, then blend.

Helio Venus in Aries: The traveling salesperson with all the glamour. The escape artist, able to leap tall buildings or scan a wall . . . amorous pursuers . . . but can escape. Bachelor/bachelorette.

Helio Venus in Taurus: The gambler who has the good sense not to. Lucky in business. May deal in foreign money. Travel agency. Love nature is enduring if there is freedom.

Hello Venus in Gemini: Another good traveling salesperson, travel agent, excellent teacher\lecturer. Love nature is more mental than physical. Could write love stories. Sagittarius imagination and Gemini pen.

Helio Venus in Cancer: Mobile homes. Airlines. Home-spun philosopher. Higher mind guidance teacher. Love nature is more emotional than physical.

Helio Venus in Leo: Pulpit orator. Leading the sheep to the alter in a royal robe. Good at industrial training. Best love nature is in foreplay. Romantic but forgetful.

Venus Rx in Capricorn

Helio Venus will be in Taurus, Gemini, Cancer, Leo or Virgo. Use any standard interpretation for Venus in Capricorn, then blend.

Helio Venus in Taurus: Represents a love for work and financial investments. No doubt owns land from an early age. Good at real estate. Love nature is steady and sincere. Expects the partner to take part in material success.

Helio Venus in Gemini: Keeps up on information pertaining to economy. Good for supervising, verbally bossy. Nature of love is serious being drawn to the intellect as well as the physical body.

Helio Venus in Cancer: Government employment is appropriate. Household alarm systems, warning devices. Love nature relates to the need to maintain security in the home and contact with loved ones.

Helio Venus in Leo: Committee chairperson, not volunteer. Executive organizational ability. Stage director. Love nature is dramatic but serious. Selective and jealous, is challenged in love.

Helio Venus in Virgo: Messages carved in stone. The rule is the rule to the letter. Corporate auditor. Land caretaker. Love nature is cool and calm, long lasting and sincere.

Venus Rx in Aquarius

Helio Venus will be in Gemini, Cancer, Leo, Virgo or Libra. Use any standard interpretation for Venus in Aquarius, then blend.

Helio Venus in Gemini: Love of creative knowledge, the unique. Money from unusual sources and at strange frequencies. Brother or sister may be best friend or employer. Love nature is rather impersonal but interesting.

Helio Venus in Cancer: Creativity in the home is a talent. Innovative when a need arises. Employment in situations of emergency. Love nature is friendly, kind, selective and loyal.

Helio Venus in Leo: Must be employed in conditions which allow creative energy to work independently and without instructions or criticisms. Love nature is warm in friendship, one friend, one lover at a time. A bit jealous.

Helio Venus in Virgo: May enjoy a pet shop or taking care of small animals. Has ability to communicate in unusual ways. Has unusual health habits such as eating schedule. Discriminating in love.

Helio Venus in Libra: Impartial diplomat. Probably psychic. Artistic in a different vein. Love nature having a need to touch and be touched but not sure who or by whom.

Venus Rx in Pisces

Helio Venus will be in Cancer, Leo, Virgo, Libra or Scorpio. Use any standard interpretation for Venus in Pisces, then blend.

Helio Venus in Cancer: Employment in a field that expresses sympathy, nurturing and protecting. May volunteer as much service as is hired out. The love nature is the kind that says "let's have a baby."

Helio Venus in Leo: Leads others out of unfortunate circumstances. May be an attorney, minister, psychologist, parent or teacher. Love nature is reciprocity—you love me, I love you.

Helio Venus in Virgo: Employment connected with healing or spiritual issues. Makes the world a better place to live. Love nature is a plea for help. Has desire to be improved.

Helio Venus in Libra: Employment should contribute to the beauty that makes the world go 'round. Love nature is pink satin sheets and sleepy music.

Helio Venus in Scorpio: Top secret on any subject will be well done. Solving the problems that have no answers. The love nature is the three "S's"—sensual, sacrificial and sexy.

Mars Retrograde in the Signs

Mars retrogrades by ten to twenty degrees, on occasion remaining in the same degree as many as twenty-three or twenty-four days when it makes the station. Since Mars is outside Earth's path around the Sun, Mars is opposite the Sun in your geocentric tropical Placidus chart. Mars is on the same side with Earth in the heliocentric chart and no more than thirty degrees from geocentric Mars. This means that, heliocentrically, Mars is in the same sign with geocentric Mars or in one of the adjoining signs. Example:

Geocentric	*Heliocentric*
27 Cancer 37 Rx	28 Gemini 44
08 Cancer 41 D	05 Leo 45

Mars rules energy and muscles. When retrograde, the individual seems to have less than normal energy for whatever sign it occupies.

Mars Rx in Aries

Helio Mars will be in Pisces, Aries or Taurus. Use any standard interpretation for Mars in Aries, then blend.

Helio Mars in Pisces: The Aries Mars is physically weakening and helio Pisces gives consent to accept the weakness. The energy should be directed toward healing others or toward self-development instead of being idle. In reference to muscles, remember to use them or lose them.

Helio Mars in Aries: This placement brings plenty of opportunity for argument, in which case the person would likely have to back down because with Mars retrograde in Aries at the peak of the period, the Sun would be in Libra, which is the sign that walks away from discord or wins with mental strategy.

Helio Mars in Taurus: Retrograde Mars in Aries practices far more patience than Mars direct in Aries, but it can tolerate only so much. The same could be said of Mars in Taurus. This combination is a double dose of patience, but the breaking point could promote serious results. The positive energy is perseverance.

Mars Rx in Taurus

Helio Mars will be in Aries, Taurus or Gemini. Use any standard interpretation for Mars in Gemini, then blend.

Helio Mars in Aries: Physical energy being low diminishes some desire to become financially active, encouraging potential to overeat or overwork. Positive energy could be determination to succeed.

Helio Mars in Taurus: Generally this double Mars in Taurus means Sun will be in Scorpio and the tendency to overspend is the danger. Scorpio, the survivor, becomes unhappy with self under such conditions. The positive energy is to learn to make solid investments and follow the quality of the two fixed signs by making fewer changes.

Helio Mars in Gemini: Knowledge is gathered on subjects that appeal to the individual. Frustration comes when one is forced to learn about topics that hold no interest. Positive energy is finding the intellectual niche and specializing in a potentially profitable area. May be an over-spender on telephones, communication equipment and pleasure on wheels.

Mars Rx in Gemini

Helio Mars will be in Taurus, Gemini or Cancer. Use any standard interpretation for Mars in Gemini, then blend.

Helio Mars in Taurus: Here is one who gets so busy working at assembly and production that the instructions are not followed, only to find the job must be repeated. Positive energy is obvious. Read the directions, just like Gemini says, and energy will not be wasted. Good for sales of quality merchandise or comfort items.

Helio Mars in Gemini: The temptation is to read too rapidly, not to comprehend, then get nervous about it. Physical energy is taxed by over talking, hyper-ventilating causing injury to the lungs. Sun most likely is in Sagittarius suggesting to get fresh air out of doors and spread knowledge. Certainly should be careful not to be overly exposed to smoke, fumes from chemicals or excessive dust.

Helio Mars in Cancer: The negative action here is to stimulate turmoil with brothers or sisters or through communications in general. Suggested positive energy is to read, write and speak the truth in a gentle tone. Advertising home products, teaching fire prevention, or home instruction courses may well be considered for livelihood or volunteer services.

Mars Rx in Cancer

Helio Mars will be in Gemini, Cancer or Leo. Use any standard interpretation for Mars in Cancer, then blend.

Helio Mars in Gemini: The danger is in talking so much, saying things over and over, that the family becomes bored. A second danger is that repeating an episode emotionally can agitate the circumstances. Positive energy meditate and learn to control the mental creativity.

Helio Mars in Cancer: The danger is emotional upsets concerning family conditions and having hurt feelings because the nurturing instinct is rejected. Sun is probably in Capricorn, which translates as work or job. Positive energy would be to become employed, nurturing those who would appreciate it. Expression of patriotism through military service or politics could be desirable.

Helio Mars in Leo: The danger is in becoming the family dictator and ending up in exile. Dramatizing emotions could become a habit. Positive energy could be found in working with children where a Leo empire could be built. It might be better to create a business-child.

Mars Rx in Leo

Helio Mars will be in Cancer, Leo or Virgo. Use any standard interpretation for Mars in Leo, then blend.

Helio Mars in Cancer: Danger is becoming distraught over not getting the best of everything, prompting one to act spoiled. Positive energy would be to truly care about other people, knowing that loving interest will be returned. There is family jealousy and little respect for women. Can be a dynamic host or hostess.

Helio Mars in Leo: Temptation to show off and get physically injured or overwork the heart. Sun is more than likely in Aquarius, implying predisposition to poor circulation and sluggish leg movements. Positive energy is to be creative, letting the product of activity be the show. Allowing others to assist, rather than expecting or demanding assistance.

Helio Mars in Virgo: Probability is to experience a heart flutter playing as a child and take care of it forever, becoming a hypochondriac because it makes a good show. Positive energy is to learn beneficial health rules, practice them daily and play not only for fun but for deeper breathing, circulation and muscular development. Walking recommended. Better to show off good-looking shoes with advantage than good-looking vehicle in declining health.

Mars Rx in Virgo

Helio Mars will be in Leo, Virgo or Libra. Use any standard interpretation for Mars in Virgo, then blend.

Helio Mars in Leo: Has a forceful knowledge of what is correct on many subjects from pool hall schedules to the protocol of coronations. A strong desire to be right and avoid embarrassment due to error. May use very strong language to get attention in groups who would accept it. Positive energy is use of good leadership abilities toward better life.

Helio Mars in Virgo: Sun is likely opposite in Pisces, attracting aggressive people who may take advantage through their impatience with native's imperfections. May have a desire for a perfect body or may neglect health consciousness altogether in believing "it can't happen to me." Puts off doing until it can be done right, and then it is often too late.

Helio Mars in Libra: May be a bit too quick to express opinion, even with the intention to be helpful. Or may go to the other extreme and hesitate too long in making a move to make improvements or changes. This placement may also belong to one who is unduly critical of partner, resulting in loneliness. Positive energy is to develop cooperative efforts.

Mars Rx in Libra

Helio Mars will be in Virgo, Libra or Scorpio. Use any standard interpretation for Mars in Libra, then blend.

Helio Mars in Virgo: Has difficulty in sharing assistance in cooperative projects. This is one who may gift wrap the garbage so it will look pretty and perfect. Never too sick to take time to look good. Seldom, or never, well enough to get dirty hands. Likes environment comfortable, pretty, clean and orderly, especially if there is a housekeeping crew. Not so willing to do it for self.

Helio Mars in Libra: Sun is most likely in Aries opposing Mars, attracting those who do not wish to be alone and who force their gentle attention. Yet there is magnetism with a give/take, push/pull contact in most relationships. Effort should be made to make firm decisions. Positive energy is to develop personal pleasure behavioral patterns. Mars rules Aries and if it opposes Sun in Libra, be careful that battles are for righteous causes and worth the price you have to pay for the fight to win. Might as well go into law. Where the talent is.

Helio Mars in Scorpio: Needs to be more selective sexually rather than give in to fear of having no relationship. In buying fewer of the things you want for yourself, you stand a better chance of having someone give you what you want. It is wise to learn all the rules about the game of credit cards or else debt could become overwhelming simply because credit was too good.

Mars Rx in Scorpio

Helio Mars will be in Libra, Scorpio or Sagittarius. Use any standard interpretation for Mars in Scorpio, then blend.

Helio Mars in Libra: Great patience is needed with co-workers. It is easier to work alone, but it is sometimes necessary to give or receive help. The chore may be less stressful if it is first decided how the cooperative energy will be shared. Remember the pleasure you receive when you do something for someone so you can allow someone to do for you. Just say "no" from the beginning when it is no deal.

Helio Mars in Scorpio: An axiom says "neither a borrower nor a lender be." It is good advice, because it is not easy to pay back, nor is it easy to collect. Much passion and anger can backlog with this energy. It is wise to clear up misunderstandings as they occur in order not to let tension collect. Hard to know to let up on the other person. They can become tense also. It is important to maintain the ability to relax.

Helio Mars in Sagittarius: Gifts flow with the luck of the Irish. You receive only to learn that you are expected to give in return or to work out the grant. Lucky to gain, but the privilege to pay is not always to your liking even though you come out best in the long run. At some point it will be necessary to settle on what you believe about spiritual issues.

Mars Rx in Sagittarius

Helio Mars will be in Scorpio, Sagittarius or Capricorn. Use any standard interpretation for Mars in Sagittarius, then blend.

Helio Mars in Scorpio: It is necessary to come face to face with spirituality and morality. What one believes about afterlife eventually is important to the individual. Carelessness is almost a habit. Could probably paper a room with speeding tickets. Not as sexual as mental unless dwelling on sex or experiencing an obsession with someone.

Helio Mars in Sagittarius: Foot-in-mouth disease is part of this placement. Say first, think later or when getting up off the floor after being knocked down. Usually speaks very loudly, argumentative without being angry. Romantically, the chase is much more fun than the catch, in fact is not so sure just what to do with a catch or when caught, depending upon who won the race.

Helio Mars in Capricorn: The business executive who is lucky enough to get out of work and get full pay but is not comfortable doing so. Travels from early in life because of need more than pleasure. May not get along well with the father because father is severely strict or father is not at home enough for his authority to be effective.

Mars Rx in Capricorn

Helio Mars will be in Sagittarius, Capricorn or Aquarius. Use any standard interpretation for Wars in Capricorn, then blend.

Helio Mars in Sagittarius: Mars is exalted in Capricorn, knowing when to act for successful results. The additional energy of Sagittarius in specialized knowledge can contribute much in excellence and quality. The potential detriment is to talk too much about what could be infringed upon. This combination would be good for business in sports equipment or sporting events organization.

Helio Mars in Capricorn: Favorite sport is work or gathering information or contacts relating to work. Making something from nothing, that is salvaging, is a pleasure and can be a method of success. A career or job that recycles or converts a natural resource or product would be of interest. Sometimes gets too busy to remember to eat. Doubtful that this individual would ever be overweight.

Helio Mars in Aquarius: Desire to use what is available (Mars Rx in Capricorn) with Mars in Aquarius could produce new, different and interesting products or creations. Creating treasures from what others may consider trash is a talent. A danger is taking advantage of friends. Caution should be taken to prevent injury to lower legs and knees.

Mars Rx in Aquarius

Helio Mars will be in Capricorn, Aquarius or Pisces. Use standard interpretations for Mars in Aquarius, then blend.

Helio Mars in Capricorn: This energy will find a way to manifest creativity but may find difficulty in developing its value to the fullest. An assistant or partner may be advisable to launch plans. The danger may be in building air castles too long and too late for large scale success. Social activity may be neglected, promoting occasions when loneliness may be experienced due to missing out on special events.

Helio Mars in Aquarius: Emphasis is on friends, social activity and new ideas. This can belong to a buddy of buddies, a party animal or a genius. In refusing to conform, the attraction is toward other non-conformists, all of whom conform by rebelling in union. Enjoys only one close friend at a time. May be a volunteer for humane activities but does not commit well for more than a moment's notice.

Helio Mars in Pisces: A soft touch for a friend. Can be overly sympathetic and allow it to be draining, both emotionally and financially. May have unusual aches and pains that are not easy to diagnose. Advised not to create trouble and to deal with issues as they occur rather than procrastinating. May be uniquely artistic.

Mars Rx in Pisces

Helio Mars will be in Aquarius, Pisces or Aries. Use any standard interpretation for Mars in Pisces, then blend.

Helio Mars in Aquarius: Worries about the strangest things! Mentally creative, especially in artistic display and color. May be strongly psychic. Has a philosophy of life that does not comply with the family creed. May be a black sheep, but is not odd if in an all black herd where a white sheep would be different. Caution: Don't let a drinking buddy drag you down (or any other negative influence).

Helio Mars in Pisces: Work with less fortunate ones where sympathy can also earn a living. Otherwise, too much time, energy and money might be given away. Lack of motivation might be a problem if surrounded by people who are always up. Needs to reach down and lift others rather than feel tread upon.

Helio Mars in Aries: "I feel sorry for me." Affirmation: "I can make me well and okay." Do something for self every day, then give away kindness and smiles. Remember: "Give a man a fish, he eats for a day; teach him to fish, he eats for a lifetime." Your retrograde Mars in Pisces taught you to fish. Your helio Mars in Aries allows you to demonstrate.

Sun-Retrograde Outer Planet Aspects

The heliocentric positions of Mercury, Venus and Mars are important to the interpretation when one of these planets is retrograde, but the positions of the outer planets do not vary greatly from geocentric to heliocentric. If the retrograde station is in one sign and the direct station in another, for a very few days of that period the retrograde planet may fall geocentrically in one sign, heliocentrically in another.

The pattern is regular. Jupiter retrogrades for roughly 120 days, about ten degrees geocentrically while moving direct, and heliocentrically about ten degrees. Note that the geocentric retrograde station is the same place of heliocentric at the direct station and that the direct station geocentrically is the same place of heliocentric at the retrograde station.

Minor Aspects

Biseptile, 102 6/7 degrees: Neptune and Pluto will experience this aspect to Sun soon following the retrograde station.

It is an energizing aspect that can contribute much to advancing projects already instigated.

Tredecile, 108 degrees: Uranus begins and closes its retrograde cycle with this aspect. Wouldn't you know! A summation of its energy could be classified as newness.

Trine, 120 degrees: A few days .after the retrograde station, the Sun and planet will be in trine aspect. A second trine will be accomplished a few days prior to the direct station. A trine is a trine is a trine, retrograde or not. Except for Mars, the outer planets are always retrograde when trine the Sun.

Sesquiquadrate, 135 degrees: The sesquiquadrate will occurs about fifteen days after the trine. Each aspect a retrograde planet makes to the Sun will occur first by separating aspect and then by applying aspect, except the opposition. The two energies of sesquiquadrate are defined as difficulties and agitation. Ever hear of converting anger to productivity? These are frustrations from a fifth or ninth house angle. The fifth supplies creativity, and the ninth supplies optimism.

Biquintile, 144 degrees: Quintile is 72 degrees and widely known as the talent aspect. Two times 72 is 144, the biquintile, which provides double talent through faith and creativity. This angle offers application of talent (216 degrees), coming from the fifth and ninth house directions. Not unfavorable vibrations from any direction. These energies promote capabilities that allow expansion from pleasures and spiritual expression.

Quincunx or Inconjunct, 150 degrees: All of the outer planets retrograde will experience the inconjunct to the Sun twice during the retrograde period. The angle is 150 degrees one way and 210 the other. You will recognize this as the work and health angle, six signs away from Aries one direction and eight signs away in the other direction. It is defined as dilemma and revision. Now what do you do in a dilemma? Turn around three times and bake cookies. And what do you do while the second batch is baking? Eat the first batch, of course. And that is why many people with Jupiter retrograde have weight problems. Jupiter has no willpower, nor does a dilemma. So you do something called work. Then you eat to settle the dilemma and the body experiences revision. Also, Jupiter rules sugar and fat; eat too much, you get sick. But we are not to get carried away with that interpretation because all of the outer planets will go through the exact aspect as the Sun transits opposing them while retrograde.

Regardless of the planetary energy, the inconjunct is the health aspect. If it is Saturn, there is too little of something, unless it is too much responsibility. Yes, we probably could work ourselves to death, but not many do. After all, the other end of this aspect is the eighth house angle.

Triseptile, 154 2/7 degrees: This aspect divides 360 degrees into seven equal parts, 51 3/7 tripled equals 154 2/7 degrees. The septile requires attention. The triseptile would be in need of more serious attention. When a chore becomes too big, we usually accept help. That is the other end of the 360 degrees, or 205 3/7. From the applying half of the retrograde period, we are on the threshold of the opposition.

Opposition, 180 degrees: Once it has been accepted that help is desirable, there are again two choices from the opposition—-separation or cooperation. At this point the retrograde term is one-half spent. There is only one opposition aspect from Sun to the retrograde planet. The planet is exactly opposite Sun and exactly conjunct Earth. Earth is between Sun and the planet.

Some astrologers maintain that any planet retrograde is adverse. My spiritual energy tells me that if we make the best of any situation it is never all bad. Perhaps the reason retrogrades appear to be adverse is because the less appealing energy of the aspects to the Sun are the separating energies which shout "change," something most of us rebel against. And, I repeat, anytime Sun is trine an outer planet, that planet is retrograde, so how then can a trine be so great? Or, if a retrograde is so adverse, does the trine not help at all? Are we to then claim that only a trine from Moon or Mars is a "good" trine, because Sun can never be trine Mercury or Venus except if they are retrograde and read heliocentrically.

Jupiter Retrograde Aspects

These interpretations will be made based upon the theory of karma, whether as in a former lifetime or limited to events in the present lifetime. Only aspects to the Sun are considered since without relativity to the Sun it would not be retrograde. Any aspect to Jupiter can be a predisposition to overindulgence.

Trine, Jupiter/Sun: In the 120 degree position, Jupiter is in a ninth house position to Sun. Gives past experiences in philosophical or religious realms, consequently holding a push-pull view of subjects. Wanting to be just, fair and honest, yet daring to flirt with borderline legalities. Might run red lights when no one is looking, borrow from the family cash register, not report all income or give shades of truth on certain scores. The 240 degree position is Jupiter just before going direct with Sun in a fifth house position from Jupiter. There are delays in courtship, romance and birth of children, possibly because of playing games with love. Both love and development of talent come in the end. Love of horses.

Sesquiquadrate, Jupiter/Sun: With Jupiter and Sun 135 degrees apart and Sun moving toward the opposition there would be difficulties in creativity, love and having children may be a task or may be separated from loved ones. Not a good placement for risk taking or gambling. You have an opportunity to learn to appreciate love. When Sun and Jupiter are 225 degrees apart, the Sun is just past the opposition aspect. One with this aspect to the Sun is advised against heavy indebtedness and to be cautious about carelessness in sexual activity and spirit communication. You have had much in past lifetimes. Now you can learn not to be greedy or envious.

Biquintile, Jupiter/Sun: With Sun applying to the opposition of Jupiter (144 degrees), can be inspirationally creative early in life. May be an entertainer. At 216 degrees, with Sun past the opposition aspect, talent for knowing the direction of economy for purpose of investments. You are learning more about giving and receiving.

Inconjunct, Jupiter/Sun: With Sun applying to the opposition to Jupiter (150 degrees), you have many activities going all the time, and don't know what to do first or next. This is the work and health aspect. Jupiter in health implies too much of something. Blood tests were created for people with Sun/Jupiter inconjunct, early detection for most anything. 210 degrees, with Sun moving away from the opposition to Jupiter, is eighth house energy and speaks of need for change and discretion where control is used. This is not a lifetime to be stubborn but to share.

Triseptile, Jupiter/Sun: At 154 2/7 degrees, Sun is moving toward the opposition to Jupiter. This is a lifetime to pay attention to people around you and to treat them with respect or be prepared to defend yourself. At 205 5/7 degrees, Sun is moving away from the opposition to Jupiter. This is a lifetime to serve, working with the forces and not being isolated.

Opposition, Jupiter/Sun, 180 degrees: You are bouncing off the ropes all your life. You may have one or many mates, and you deal with numerous people. Most every contact seems to be important. You are learning to get along with others. The sooner you get it right, the more fun you can have.

Saturn Retrograde Aspects

Saturn represents the past and things of long standing. Saturn also represents lessons to be learned. Any retrograde in the natal chart is said to indicate repetition and unfinished business. Saturn is practical and builds slowly. Only aspects to the Sun are considered.

Tredecile, Saturn /Sun: At 108 degrees, the aspect between Saturn and Sun is within one degree at the retrograde station. The energy of the angle urges the native to begin construction and to lay a foundation. Saturn uses that which has little or no use to the average person. It is similar to the Eskimo igloos made of ice blocks. Nowhere else in the world but Alaska are buildings made of ice (and of course modernization has replaced that). At 252 degrees, Sun has gone through all its aspects to Saturn retrograde by the time this aspect is formed and much has been experienced. Now is the time of recognition of potential and ability. The native with this aspect from Sun to Saturn has self-awareness.

Trine, Saturn/Sun: At 120 degrees, this aspect is a picture of the willingness to walk away from responsibility. Work has little or no pleasure because the niche will not be found until later in life when the native learns that work is a way for all. At 240 degrees, Sun has past the opposition and soon will turn direct. The energy seeks worthwhile activity. Somehow it has been learned that nobody takes care of your business like you do.

Sesquiquadrate, Saturn/Sun: At 135 degrees, everything has a price and sometimes taxes on top of that! You are learning about right and wrong. That's why you get caught when you err. At 225 degrees, every day is another test in patience. Clench your fists, tense your body and relax. Try not to let your irritation show and they will let up on you.

Biquintile, Saturn/ Sun: At 144 degrees, Saturn gives what you deserve. You have ability to make big bucks but you need to know the money rules, abide by honesty and work. At 216 degrees, take aptitude tests, search your mind for your talents, remember all the compliments you have received for what you have done well in, find your niche and fit into it.

Inconjunct, Saturn/Sun: At 150 degrees, your personal assignment for a happy life this round is work. It is good for your health and your pocketbook and great for your soul's growth. Hang in there! (Also see Saturn under health in this book.) At 210 degrees, many changes are seemingly forced on you, but you need them for your spiritual uplifting. There are times if you were not forced to change you would miss some great opportunities. No doubt if you think back you can remember that you lost a job and thought your world was over, just to get a better job. You were stuck before. The universe moved you.

Triseptile, Saturn/ Sun: At 154 2\7 degrees, people are always giving you a rough time. Stop and consider how they feel about what you do to them. It could change your whole life. At 205 5/7 degrees, the saying, "you scratch my back and I'll scratch yours" is a good one to remember. It's called reciprocity. Service exchange, that is. You are learning not to be all take and no give.

Opposition, Saturn/Sun, 180 degrees: You came into this life looking for someone to tell you what to do when. You want authority in companionship, someone who has smarts. The sooner you realize this person will probably be older than you, the sooner you can get on with it. This is one who laughs less, but you can laugh with others.

Uranus Retrograde Aspects

If you have Uranus retrograde and dislike surprises, you might learn why right here. Uranus is originality, inventive ability. Maybe the universe keeps telling you to be a genius with what you have or it might be taken away.

Tredecile, Uranus/Sun: At 108 degrees, you have all the ingredients for starting something important. Use it or lose it. Take stock as to whether you have been too extravagant, which is definitely a Uranian word. At 252 degrees, learn as you go. Most physical labors are as much in the doing as in the instructions. Nobody learns to ride a bicycle sitting on a lawn chair.

Trine, Uranus/Sun: At 120 degrees, you have great creative ability. The problem is you might have too much. Trines do that to us. Doing one thing at a time might be boring for you but that is about all most of us can manage. You can have more than one project going at a time; work on one and then the other. Your genius is very mental. At 240 degrees, you have the kind of genius that can take three sticks and build a castle, probably because you would use one for a dowsing rod and find steel beams. New romances any time you need excitement. Did the dowsing rod find that too?

Sesquiquadrate, Uranus/Sun: At 135 degrees, you get an unexpected bonus check in the mail and the next envelope has a bill in it for an equal amount. The lesson you are learning is to be prepared for anything and spend only what you have in hand. At 225 degrees, it seems like every time you have a day off, somebody else needs it for something you feel obligated to do. Talent and service go hand in hand in your life. Enjoying what you do is important.

Biquintile, Uranus/Sun: At 144 degrees, the product or job you got might not have been what you wanted, but you found it was more valuable in the long run. When you were little, they took your old toys to give you more appropriate ones. At 216 degrees, you wanted to stay home but went to a movie with a friend and saw someone you had been wanting to see for a long time. That is how this aspect serves you. Things are forever happening for the better when you thought it was a lost cause, if you accept the changes.

Inconjunct, Uranus/Sun: At 150 degrees, people sure enjoy volunteering your services. You have a lifetime to learn to say "no." The earlier you begin, the sooner you can master it. The time you give away will be more meaningful to you if you choose the schedule. At 210 degrees, you are learning to modernize every phase of your life. You must have spent many lifetimes in ancient history, and you brought with you an exciting sense of survival.

Triseptile, Uranus/Sun: At 154 2/7 degrees, people come into your life just when you need them most. The art is in learning when to let them go. You must. not own another person. At 205 5/7 degrees, other people fill your life with friendship; if not, you don't need them. Learn to accept the other person's right to impulsiveness and freedom.

Opposition, Uranus/ Sun, 180 degrees: You attract restless people as potential partners or mates. The way to hold them is to allow them freedom. You may be married or mated many times. Certain to experience at least one relationship that begins in a flash and ends just as quickly. Face each new relationship as a new learning opportunity and as a new friend. For you, friends are better lovers. Lovers are jealous.

Neptune Retrograde Aspects

Neptune is considered primarily adverse energy but only because we fail to apply the spirituality of its energy. This planet helps us put worries aside, but the negative application is to reach out for something to worry about. Then, once found, to try to destroy the cause. This is the kind of thinking that turns to drugs, alcohol, tranquilizers, lies and any other source to destroy the discomfort that grows out of worry.

Positive Neptune recognizes the condition, does what can be done and lets go. Neptune is faith to trust universal power to work. The Biblical definition of faith, from Hebrews 11:1, is: ". . .the substance of things hoped for, the evidence of things not seen." You don't have to be religious to use a universal truth. Many problems would be mysteriously solved if we would just let the universe handle it.

Biseptile, Neptune/Sun: At 102 6/7 degrees, inspiration comes but you need more knowledge. You are learning the value of using knowledge. Knowledge is a great joy for you, but when you get to the end of the course you may find the field is closed. Spiritual guidance can be helpful in your ventures; otherwise, you could become a perpetual student going nowhere. At 257 1/7 degrees, an idea is born. You are filled with excitement. You share it with another. Others take your ideas and make them work, and you are left out. Why? Probably because you allowed it to be no more than an idea. Thoughts become things, but it usually takes physical application to make them work. Try supporting your brainchild rather than letting it out for adoption.

Tredecile, Neptune/Sun: At 108 degrees, you can't build a chimney from the top without faith, which can positively defy gravity! You are here to learn the value of faith. Test it, then use it. You'll like it. At 252 degrees, playing the field in romance is a game with you and you're continually disappointed. You are here to learn that beauty comes from within. Once you see the inner light of the one you love, you will know that love is not all sex.

Trine, Neptune/Sun: At 120 degrees, this is a terrific aspect for musical talent, dancing, art. crafting and color therapy through theme and form. You could be a spiritual healer. You are advised to avoid drugs, alcohol, etc. because it is easy to give in to a destructive habit. At 240 degrees, your message is the same as 120 degrees, but you may have to become aware of the spirit world using your energy in a negative way.

Sesquiquadrate, Neptune/Sun: At 135 degrees, although you see it, it's not rally what you see because Neptune rules mirrors. Your lesson in life is to take a good look at self to eliminate errors. The 225 degree aspect is like having a hole in your pocket. Whatever you stash away falls through. The lesson is, double-line your pockets. Take precautions.

Biquintile, Neptune/Sun: At 144 degrees, your purpose in this lifetime may be as a spiritual leader to promote happiness, or you may find your best place is an entertainer to lighten the load for the world. At the least, you can enjoy your own optimism. At 216 degrees, you could be psychic, but you are to be selective about your spirit guides. You could get one who was an old drinking buddy from a past life instead of your most inspirational pastor, priest or rabbi.

Inconjunct, Neptune/Sun, At 150 degrees, you probably know your route to the hospital better than to any other place on earth. You are so compassionate. The danger is that you can borrow every pain the patient feels. If you can take it psychically you can release it psychically, simply decide to refuse it. Be a ray of sunshine but not a bacteria wastebasket. At 210 degrees, you could be a spiritual healer. Surely you often wonder why so many mentally undernourished people find their way to you. You can help them. You have inner feelings for the helpless and confused and they know it. Your lesson in this life is to be understanding. But it does not mean you have to spend all your time with people who drain your sympathies and emotions.

Triseptile, Neptune/Sun: At 154 2/7 degrees, there is a strong chance that you are in the presence of chemicals or fumes several hours a week. You are advised to be aware of the potential dangers of such an environment. Ink is a chemical often overlooked as a threat. You nay also have allergies to something you would not consider an enemy. Find them. Tell it that it has no power over you and believe what you say. The 205 5/7 degree aspect from Sun to Neptune reminds me of a conversation with a woman several years back who had a parallel situation in her chart and asked, "What kind of person would Neptune in the seventh house marry?" My answer: "A minister, an artist, an alcoholic." Her reply: "You're right. I've been married three times and in that order." She proved you don't have to settle on them being alike. Right?

Opposition, Neptune/Sun: If this aspect is 180 degrees, read the above paragraph (205 5/7 degrees); it applies here also. In addition, realize that you attract people who need guidance and depend greatly upon your strength. The challenge for your life is to be the best of whatever you are. You may be the best person that someone knows. Does that give you consciousness? Neptune rules the subconscious and, as long as you keep it clean, there should be no problem.

Pluto Retrograde Aspects

Though Moon governs minor and daily change in our lives, the major shakeups come by way of Pluto, when emotions long collected within will finally reach an escape point. Pluto retrograde will hold those emotions even more securely and secretively. Both the evolution and the revolution can be extreme. This tiny little planet so far away may be likened unto atomic energy. Some astrologers deny that Pluto can even share energy on our planet, but an open mind can only conclude that its strength is dynamic. Pluto transforms. Think of the butterfly. It is first a larva, then it goes in hiding to transform and emerge with wings. Pluto does that kind of transformation. You may have heard someone say, "When we first met we detested each other until we fell in love." Then we all know the love birds who divorced in total hatred. Pluto harbored emotions and emerged transformed.

Biseptile, Pluto/Sun: Enthusiasm describes the 102 6/7 degree aspect. Do something or bust! If it is romantic, it's probably in lust rather than in love. Of course, if it is right, it might emerge as love later. Major change in lifestyle at some point. Usually indicates separation from a parent early in life.

Independence at a young age. With the 257 1/7 degree angle, the emotion and awareness are there, but spiritual balance must be weighed. An important business deal would be investigated if there were any suspicions concerning fairness.

Tredecile, Pluto/Sun: With the 108 degree aspect, you are able to pick up the pieces after an upset. Can build back even better than before. Will need at some time to rebuild the home because of destruction or loss or because of family breakup. At 252 degrees, you don't have to be hit in the head to see the light. At an early age you are, as Helen Keller said when she first understood her teacher's explanation of God, "I always knew there was such a One." Nobody had to tell you either.

Trine, Pluto/Sun: At 120 degrees, leadership so powerful that it could be dangerous if following a destructive avenue. Your children may be afraid of you because of the power of authority. Very persuasive. If you have the 240 degree aspect, you have the ability to be an outstanding spiritual leader. Strong in political circles with qualities to be an excellent courtroom attorney. Good for teaching courses that reconstruct the world in form or in philosophy.

Sesquiquadrate, Pluto/Sun: At 135 degrees, people feel threatened by your power. Good for sports and physical demonstrations. Not the best for romance and parenthood unless you have learned to tone down energy. With the 225 degree aspect, you get frustrated and angry if money deals get out of order. Difficulty in handling rejection. Not wise to be a lender. Don't know your own strength.

Biquintile, Pluto/Sun. At 144 degrees, can come out the winner on a blind date. Unplanned change can put you in a far more advantageous set of circumstances. With the 216 degree aspect, you can be powerfully psychic. A financial tycoon through investments is a potential.

Inconjunct, Pluto/Sun: With 150 degrees, much physical strength. Can mend quickly following illness or surgery. Is given the heavy work on the job. With 210 degrees, there may come a time when you are required to change or die. Not wise to let stubbornness take your life.

Triseptile, Pluto/Sun: With 154 2/7 degrees, you need to learn to strike a bargain in work and trade favors, or you get the work while others get the bargain. Others are as much an advantage to you as you are to them, but if they are not sharing with you, they may not value your services. At 205 5/7 degrees, you look for important and powerful people only to find that they overpower you. That's okay so long as you are willing to be VP and not top dog. You may have been a king in another lifetime and now you are learning to be a peasant.

Opposition, Pluto/Sun: The 180 degree aspect brings people who pressure you into your environment. Always know that they will not push you around if you don't allow it. Many people with this aspect have been taken advantage of sexually because they think they have to submit to power. Too many times a parent was the first offender.

Health and Retrograde Planets

The inconjunct is the health aspect and every planet engages that aspect to the Sun when retrograde, except Mercury and Venus. Even that can be discounted when it is taken into consideration that the heliocentric view gives even those two the same angles as the outer planets when retrograde.

Since retrograde planets seem to figure so prominently in health and wellness, it may be of great benefit to take a closer look at each of the planets and how they relate to the physical body. As stated before, it is the aspect to the Sun which is the vitality, that contributes to the importance of the inconjunct from Sun to the retrograde planet.

Mercury in Health

Mercury rules the nervous system. As the ruler of Gemini, Mercury governs hands, arms, shoulders, lungs and all respiratory organs and functions. As the ruler of Virgo, Mercury governs the intestines and bowels. The mind and at least some portions of the brain undoubtedly react to Mercury. Some authorities say that Mercury co-rules the thyroid. An aspect between Mercury and Saturn relates to hearing. If

Mercury is retrograde in the natal chart, there seems to be some degree of malfunction to one more of these.

Mercury retrograde at birth will progress direct by or before age twenty-three at the very latest and there will be noticeable improvement to whatever is out of order, even if nothing medical has been done to correct the malfunction.

Mercury bodily disorders many times are not what would be medical problems, but are of the mind in that the nervous system is subject to the mind unless there is a physical pressure. It's true that medicine can relax the mind, but it will not remain repaired unless the thinking is revamped.

Mercury Rx in Aries or in the first house: There may be nervous twitching about the face, especially near the eyes.

Mercury Rx in Taurus or in the second house: The voice may reflect differently under nervous stress or there may be a direct relativity to thyroid in this instance.

Mercury Rx in Gemini or in the third house: The thinking process may be interrupted or delayed, but it does not necessarily imply a lower IQ. Hands or arms may be weak. There may be susceptibility to pneumonia or bronchial conditions. Wise to avoid smoking, fumes from chemicals and airborne particles such as pollen and dust.

Mercury Rx in Cancer or in the fourth house: The nervous stomach, difficulty in eating under stress.

Mercury Rx in Leo or in the fifth house: The heart flutters under stress. Leo rules the spine, and discomfort of the back and spine may occur when nervous.

Mercury Rx in Virgo or in the sixth house: Diarrhea may occur when under stress, in which case it is not unusual for constipation to follow. Needs to guard against infections of the intestines.

Mercury Rx in Libra or in the seventh house: Involuntary kidney action may occur when under stress, or kidneys may temporarily cease to function.

Mercury Rx in Scorpio or in the eighth house: Bladder control is difficult when under stress. The menstrual cycle may be altered. Males may find difficulty in performing or maintaining an erection.

Mercury Rx in Sagittarius or in the ninth house: Cramps in the upper legs, thighs or hips may be a problem.

Mercury Rx in Capricorn or in the tenth house: Quivering knees, especially when called upon to speak in public.

Mercury Rx in Aquarius or in the eleventh house: Tricky ankles or cramps in the ankles. Nervousness in the calves of the legs.

Mercury Rx in Pisces or in the twelfth house: Cramps in the feet. May promote reoccurring problems with formation of mucous at some other area.

Venus in Health

Venus rules kidneys, ovaries, throat, voice box, veins, puberty, sperm, ova, sex acts, touch, venereal diseases, at least a part of the function of the thyroid and most likely the lymphatic system.

No great claims have been made that Venus rules hair, but when Venus is retrograde in the natal chart, the native tends to have hair that is coarse. It is not easy to separate some of these as to which is subject to Taurus and which is to be assigned to Libra.

Venus Rx in Aries or in the first house: The skin shows blemishes and may feel rough, and the hair is coarse. The native is a bit aggressive and may be subject to injury.

Venus Rx in Taurus or in the second house: Sore throat and tonsilitis may be more frequent than with other people. Sore throat not connected with colds, post nasal drainage or local irritation may be a signal that the reproductive organs are not functioning normally.

Venus Rx in Gemini or in the third house: May not find pleasure in using the hands in craft works.

Venus Rx in Cancer or in the fourth house: The stomach may reject sweets. Could have delays in childbirth and not be able to breast feed.

Venus Rx in Leo or in the fifth house: Leo is the lover. The heart can truly hurt when love does not go smoothly.

Venus Rx in Virgo or in the sixth house: May experience ruptured veins in the abdominal area.

Venus Rx in Libra or in the seventh house: Almost certainly will have ovarian problems, if female. In the male, sperm count may be low. Both subject to kidney irritations.

Venus Rx in Scorpio or in the eighth house: Warned to be very cautious about exposure to venereal diseases.

Venus Rx in Sagittarius or in the ninth house: Varicose veins a strong potential.

Venus Rx in Capricorn or in the tenth house: May experience bone deformities.

Venus Rx in Aquarius or in the eleventh house: Swollen ankles from kidney problems very likely.

Venus Rx in Pisces or in the twelfth house: There are reflex points from all over the body on the feet. They are sensitive to touch and will become sore at reflex points.

Mars in Health

Mars is hot and rules temperature. If Mars is retrograde, the normal temperature is usually lower than the 98.6 average. Mars also rules muscles and energy. Mars retrograde seems to lessen the energy level, and there will be a weak muscle somewhere in the body, usually indicated by sign or house placement of Mars. Mars also rules the eyes, head, sinuses to some degree, nose, male sex organs, surgery, scars, hives, blisters, sharp pain, gall and injuries.

Keeping active is very important in order to support the muscular system. Even the lightest exercise is better than no movement. Walk, walk, walk. Walking uses practically every muscle in the body and without strain. Best not to take the easiest way. Not parking in the nearest available space is healthy.

Mars Rx in Aries: The more passive energy as a result of Mars Rx slows blood flow to the head and headaches result. It is important to keep the hands and feet warm to encourage continuous flow of blood. There is generally a scar on the face or head. Potential for eye and sinus problems.

Mars Rx in Taurus or in the second house: Potential injury to the neck or sore throat are not unusual.

Mars Rx in Gemini or in the third house: Muscular depletion to hands, arms, and shoulders. Lack of energy to breathe when experiencing respiratory illnesses.

Mars Rx in Cancer or in the fourth house: Low stomach acid. Lax muscle in the breasts.

Mars Rx in Leo or in the fifth house: Heart muscles weak. More walking helpful. Hay have weak back muscles.

Mars Rx in Virgo or in the sixth house: Sluggish intestines may cause constipation. Abdominal massage suggested to stimulate blood flow and energize muscles.

Mars Rx in Libra or in the seventh house - Focus is on kidneys. Much liquid needed to keep body fluids circulating. Sexual activity is an advantage but not if promiscuous. Resistance to sexual disease is low.

Mars Rx in Scorpio or in the eighth house: Lax muscular system. Surgery to sex organs. Males may be slow or short term in erection, but healthy sexual activity. Deep-seated emotions contribute to gall bladder problems. Hemorrhoids.

Mars Rx in Sagittarius or in the ninth house: Likely injury to thighs or hips. Secret to locating health problems is blood test. Blood pressure may be a factor.

Mars Rx in Capricorn or in the tenth house: Possible broken bones as indicated by Mars by sign and house. Nails and teeth may be soft.

Mars Rx in Aquarius or in the eleventh house: Potential injury to ankles or weak lower legs and ankles. Nerve fluids may be distorted in some manner.

Mars Rx in Pisces or in the twelfth house: Possible injury to feet or weak arches. Shoes rub blisters.

Jupiter in Health

Jupiter rules the hips, thighs, liver, blood, growths, tumors, philosophy of life and optimism. Motivation and attitude relate strongly to the general health of one with Jupiter retrograde. Attitudes on giving and receiving and indulgences are major in health for Jupiter retrograde (or direct, for that matter).

Jupiter Rx in Aries or in the first house: Growths on the face or head. Blood pressure or blood sugar may be a source of affliction.

Jupiter Rx in Taurus or in the second house: Growth on the neck or throat or thyroid condition may need attention.

Jupiter Rx in Gemini or in the third house: Blood circulation in hands, arms and across shoulders may need stimulation. Massages would be helpful. Breathing exercises recommended.

Jupiter Rx in Cancer or in the fourth house: Malfunction of liver may interfere with digestion. Does not make breasts larger, but may contribute to potential of growths in breasts.

Jupiter Rx in Leo or in the fifth house: A desire for rich foods contributes to liver disorders and heart problems, which encourage internal growths.

Jupiter Rx in Virgo or in the sixth house: Interference with blood flow in the abdominal area. Sometimes due to over doses of food supplements.

Jupiter Rx in Libra or in the seventh house: Impurities settled in kidneys. May develop growths on ovaries. Skin blemishes from liver variances may occur.

Jupiter Rx in Scorpio or in the eighth house: Annual checkup on condition of sex organs recommended after thirty-five. Possible growths in area of sex organs. Long term neglect in constipation may contribute to serious problems with hemorrhoids.

Jupiter Rx in Sagittarius or in the ninth house: Lack of

physical and spiritual exercise. A more dedicated practice of spiritual faith will heal much. Blood sugar and blood pressure both potentially hazardous.

Jupiter Rx in Capricorn or in the tenth house: Bone joints are the focus of weakness. Misplaced teeth may also be a problem.

Jupiter Rx in Aquarius or in the eleventh house: Any injury to the lower legs should be well attended because of the sensitivity to blood clotting in that area.

Jupiter Rx in Pisces or in the twelfth house: This is philosophical. Prayer is the best healer and illness prevention. But if it fails look to the liver and over indulgence.

Saturn in Health

Saturn rules bones, nails, teeth, acids, constipation, stagnation, sluggishness, deficiencies, body minerals, aging process, rheumatism, arthritis, skin, and any solidification, such as hardening of the arteries.

It is said that more than eighty percent of all health disorders begin in the colon. Most of this can be traced to Saturn. Diet is important, getting sufficient (not being deficient) acids and minerals. Good teeth allow for sufficient (not deficient) chewing of food for better digestion helping to prevent constipation. Age does not show as much if one is healthy. Organic functions are more normal. Most of this is based on Saturn rulerships. We may play around with the other planets, but when Saturn shows up in the health chart, pay attention whether it is retrograde or direct.

Saturn Rx in Aries or in the first house: Tooth tartar as a result of wrong acids or wrong amounts of certain acids. Granulated eyelids may require care.

Saturn Rx in Taurus or in the second house: Stiff neck or teeth of the lower law may collect tartar.

Saturn Rx in Gemini or in the third house: Labored breathing from poor circulation or too little body movement.

Saturn Rx in Cancer or in the fourth house: Incorrect diet is most of the issue in this case.

Saturn Rx in Leo or in the fifth house: Heart or back problems arising out of worry about children or romances. Unless it is an ego issue.

Saturn Rx in Virgo or in the sixth house: Strong chance of overdoing food supplements, in which case there may be a surplus or deficiency of a mineral. Even if not food supplements, the natural order of eating is probably out of balance.

Saturn Rx in Libra or in the seventh house: Kidney sediments, stones, or old blood stored up in or around the female organs.

Saturn Rx in Scorpio or in the eighth house: Abused or neglected sex organs. Colon needs to be kept clean to help prevent hemorrhoids.

Saturn Rx in Sagittarius or in the ninth house: Bone injury to legs. Attitude is important for good health. Learning the art of giving and receiving can be helpful.

Saturn Rx in Capricorn or in the tenth house: Usually needs exercise which moves the parts of the body not used in work routine. General body sluggishness.

Saturn Rx in Aquarius or in the eleventh house: If standing too long has been the cause of problem, may need to elevate feet in order to encourage better circulation to the ankles and calves.

Saturn Rx in Pisces or in the twelfth house: Tired feet. Keep feet warm and elevate them frequently. May promote corns.

Uranus in Health

Uranus rules the unusual in health, those things which occur suddenly, such as an attack of appendicitis. The unbearable pain comes suddenly, but the thorn has been a long time in the growing. Other topics under the rulership of Uranus are adultery, convulsions, allergies, viruses, spasms, radiation, electric shock, epilepsy, out of joints, paralysis and, in some situations, accidents.

Uranus brings the sudden and unexpected, but if the extenuating circumstances are studied it will be found that the individual is making a bid for freedom of or from life or a bid for attention.

Uranus Rx in Aries or in the first house: Head banging may accompany some of the above list of rulerships, epilepsy, convulsions, etc. Allergies on the face or head may be a problem.

Uranus Rx in Taurus or in the second house: Sudden loss of voice may relate to this position also viruses bringing sore throat.

Uranus Rx in Gemini or in the third house: Spasms or sudden nervous attacks identify with this energy, also allergies and hyperventilation.

Uranus Rx in Cancer or in the fourth house: Viruses accompanied by vomiting are common. Sudden attacks and spasms of the stomach when under emotional stress are not unusual. Problems with breasts.

Uranus Rx in Leo or in the fifth house: Almost uncontrollable sexual urges may occur. Epilepsy may be a potential.

Uranus Rx in Virgo or in the sixth house: Intestinal disorders due to nervousness, diarrhea, spastic colon or appendicitis.

Uranus Rx in Libra or in the seventh house: Unusual disorders related to the female organs in women and sudden attacks related to kidneys or liver (jaundice.) in both men and women.

Uranus Rx in Scorpio or in the eighth house: Sudden attacks that are difficult to diagnose many of which are contracting muscles.

Uranus Rx in Sagittarius or in the ninth house: An attack of sciatica interrupting motivation. Unusual disorders of the blood.

Uranus Rx in Capricorn or in the tenth house: The trick knee speaks out off schedule. An abscessed tooth yells.

Uranus Rx in Aquarius or in the eleventh house: Strange things that happen suddenly to prevent the native doing what they did not want to do in the first place.

Uranus Rx in Pisces or in the twelfth house: Mucous will develop in unusual places in the body. Strange disorders of the feet.

Neptune in Health

There are three main topics under the rulership of Neptune: sleep, alcoholism and toxins and, in that order, one has trouble sleeping, takes alcohol and retains toxins. Other Neptune-ruled subjects related to health are yeast, drugs, medication, anything false, mental attitude and bloating, plus problems relating to the feet.

Another major illness related to Neptune is compounding medication. People just fail to tell one doctor what is being given by another, and mixing chemistry in the body causes adverse effects. Additional conditions occur when medication is continued for years after the ailment has left, so the body creates another ailment if one is determined to medicate something.

Anything false is ruled by Neptune. This would cover teeth, implants, artificial hands, arms, legs, or fingernails.

Neptune Rx in Aries or in the first house: Possible skin conditions from cosmetics or soap.

Neptune Rx in Taurus or in, the second house: Smoking or allergy to some food being swallowed may be the offender.

Neptune Rx in Gemini or in the third house: Breathing offending chemicals or being exposed to smoke or dust could be damaging.

Neptune Rx in Cancer or in the fourth house: This is very possibly a chemical reaction from medication or improper food combining.

Neptune Rx in Leo or in the fifth house: False modesty does not allow the individual to take good care of self, such as being embarrassed to go to the bathroom or not wanting others to know there is anything wrong.

Neptune Rx in Virgo or in the sixth house: This one uses the body for a chemistry laboratory and is retaining toxins in the intestines, or has parasites. Neptune being the unknown inhabitants.

Neptune Rx in Libra or in the seventh house: The great error here is thinking that tomorrow it will be okay but it is difficult to catch tomorrow.

Neptune Rx in Scorpio or in the eighth house: Unawareness that there may be a problem and not wanting anyone to know, can harbor a disease.

Neptune Rx in Sagittarius or in the ninth house: Any problem will no doubt have a spiritual foundation. But will be found in the blood. (Sound like a Christian persuasion?)

Neptune Rx in Capricorn or in the tenth house: This is a refusal to accept that there is anything wrong or takes the reverse energy and takes advantage of the opportunity to be waited on.

Neptune Rx in Aquarius or in the eleventh house: Toxins, like fluids, seek a lower level. This means that the toxins here settle in the lower legs and become difficult to remove.

Neptune Rx in Pisces or in the twelfth house: Toxins hide in any spot, especially in the feet. Trouble sleeping. May like being the patient.

Pluto in Health

Pluto rules some strange ailments but let us begin by saying that Pluto, especially when retrograde, in any sign, seems to have a powerful ability to restore to good health.

Some topics ruled by Pluto that relate to health are odors, reproductive organs, rectum, decay, brutality, poison and venom.

The part of the body where Pluto is found tends to deteriorate before other parts. The retrograde keeps warning us so we can take care of it. Pluto direct does not.

Pluto Rx in the first house: May have decaying teeth, falling hair or severe sinus problems.

Pluto Rx in the second house: May have bad tonsils.

Pluto Rx in the third house: Reoccurring respiratory conditions.

Pluto Rx in the fourth house: Ulcers reoccurring. Problems with breasts.

Pluto Rx in the fifth house: Heart ailments reoccur.

Pluto Rx in the sixth house: Colon requires attention.

Pluto Rx in the seventh house: Kidneys require care.

Pluto Rx in the eighth house: Care of the reproductive organs needed.

Pluto Rx in the ninth house: Special care of the liver needed.

Pluto Rx in the tenth house: Bone damage has need for proper minerals.

Pluto Rx in the eleventh house: Dehydration seems to be a problem.

Pluto Rx in the twelfth house: A breakdown of body tissue needs care.

Progressed and Transiting Retrograde Planets

The workshop my students seem to enjoy more than any other is when they take the ephemeris and find their birth date and count one day for a year forward until they come to a planet that is changing direction that year. The date of birth is year zero. The following day represents age one and so on.

After they have found all the changes from birth to the present, they go back to the birth date and go in the other direction, conversely, and talk about each of the planets that have changed direction. In all the years we have done that, never yet have we had anyone who didn't have a planet change direction.

Get your ephemeris. Find your birth date, which is year zero. Look for the first planet you find changing direction. How old were you? What happened that was appropriate to the energy of the planet, sign and house?

Then go back to the birth date, counting it as zero and the previous day as age one, and count backward. List all the planets that have changed direction.

For many years people told me that secondary progressions (forward) only described events, and that the converse progressions (backward) dealt only with inner feelings. This has not been my experience. Both leave impressions whether events or thoughts. The examples below illustrate this.

Mercury

Mercury converse direct in ninth, rules ninth; went deeply into organized church.

Mercury converse retrograde in ninth, rules ninth; plunged into metaphysics.

Mercury converse retrograde in tenth, rules first and tenth; married.

Mercury progressed direct in Cancer in eleventh; started going to church.

Mercury converse retrograde in eleventh, rules seventh; first boyfriend.

Mercury progressed retrograde, end of eighth, in Pisces; husband died.

Mercury converse direct in seventh, rules eighth; sexually abused by stepfather.

Mercury progressed direct in eighth, rules ninth; accident, spiritual awareness.

Numerous instances where progressed Mercury changed direction within one year of marriage.

Venus

Venus converse retrograde in ninth, rules first and eighth; new job with constant training.

Venus progressed direct in eighth, rules eighth and first; quit loving husband and quit giving husband money.

Venus progressed retrograde in tenth, rules second and ninth; quit wife and job.

Venus progressed direct on Ascendant, rules second and converse ninth; in love, legal order to be supported.

Venus converse direct in eleventh, rules second and seventh; partner stopped supporting, had to go to work

Mars

Mars progressed retrograde third cusp, rules tenth, conjunct Jupiter; opened book store, energy depletion, malignant growth under arm.

Mars progressed retrograde in seventh, rules converse second; married to support husband who abused her.

Mars progressed direct in third, rules eighth, in Sagittarius; quit gambling.

Mars converse retrograde in third, rules eighth, in Sagittarius; started playing stock market.

Mars converse direct in first, rules seventh; started having affairs.

Jupiter

Jupiter converse direct in first, rules second and ninth; joined air force.

Jupiter converse retrograde in second, in Scorpio, rules third; near death, learned to read at age three.

Jupiter converse direct in ninth, rules first; started college.

Jupiter progressed retrograde in ninth, rules fifth; self education on college level.

Jupiter progressed direct in seventh, rules tenth; formed partnership.

Several instances of drastic weight gain associated with Jupiter changing direction conversely.

Saturn

Saturn progressed retrograde in eighth, rules second; husband financially dependent, mental problems.

Saturn progressed retrograde in Leo in seventh, rules third; moved in with older woman.

Saturn converse direct in tenth, rules seventh; partners insisted that he become responsible for his business.

Saturn converse retrograde in fifth in Taurus, rules second; age four, started very valuable card collection.

Uranus

Uranus converse retrograde in twelfth, rules ninth; reluctantly quit college.

Uranus converse direct in fifth, rules third; desire to return to hometown to live.

Uranus progressed retrograde in fourth, rules seventh; became bisexual.

Uranus progressed direct in eleventh, rules ninth; age seven, met lifelong friend.

Neptune

Neptune progressed retrograde in Scorpio in third, rules seventh; raped by brother.

Neptune converse retrograde in ninth house, rules third; started study of metaphysics.

Neptune converse direct in twelfth, rules fourth; reluctantly moved away from home.

Pluto

Pluto progressed direct in seventh, in Leo, rules tenth; sent to prep school.

Pluto converse retrograde in second, rules fifth; rheumatic fever.

Pluto converse direct in eleventh, rules third; first of many attempts to commit suicide.

Pluto progressed retrograde in third, rules sixth; major respiratory illness.

Transiting Retrograde Planets

Retrogrades by transit usually mean that things relating to the planet, house and sign will go on hold or be temporarily interrupted. Let's say you are decorating your home and Neptune goes retrograde in Capricorn in your fourth house. Your decorating may be delayed due to the unavailability of the paint you want. Neptune is paint. Capricorn is the paint company or store. Your home is the fourth house.

Now, assume you have planned a very special trip and Venus makes a retrograde station in your ninth house just prior to your planned departure. Air line strike? Your third house rules Venus and your sister who has been out of the country for five years unexpectedly comes home. You plan to buy a car and a planet goes retrograde in your eighth house. The bank puts a bind on loans temporarily.

How about changing direction direct? Say you have always wanted to go to Las Vegas and thought you could last year, but missed. Then Jupiter makes a direct station in your fifth house of pleasure, releasing the interruption and you're off.

Pretend Saturn went retrograde in your third house and moved back into your second, where it made a direct station. You get a really good job. Second house Saturn gives substantial money that works for you. Of course the former Saturn retrograde station in your third may mean you got your brother's job and he doesn't like you any more.

In horary studies, planets stay in motion. If the question is ruled by a planet that is retrograde at the time of the question, the condition will change when the planet goes direct. If the ruling planet is direct and will soon turn retrograde, the situation asked about may not develop or it will alter. Retrograde planets in horary bring things and people back. For example: Will my husband come back home? Yes, Neptune rules the seventh and is retrograde in the fourth, but he won't be the same and will act strange.

Retrograde Mercury contracts change in content or a mortgage may be sold to another lender.

Retrograde Mercury writings are reprinted.

Marry when Venus is retrograde, and somebody falls out of oive.

A car bought with Mars retrograde gets scars.

Jupiter retrograde, big deals bomb out but you can make a rerun on a good trip.

Saturn retrograde can bring back old acquaintances and karmic contacts.

How can one predict what Uranus retrograde will suddenly, uninvited and unexpectedly hold? Anything from an accident to winning the lottery, provided you've won before.

If spiritual growth, psychic development or day dreaming is on the agenda, look forward to good results. If a realistic new venture carved in stone with great success is the order, you may be at the movies. You might as well get used to it because Neptune is retrograde almost half the year.

Pluto is the reconstructor. Direct builds from the outside. Example: The top dictator. Retrograde builds from within. Example: I change me. Pluto retrograde is terrific for self healing, whether in the natal chart or by transit.

www.ingramcontent.com/pod-product-compliance
Lightning Source LLC
Chambersburg PA
CBHW032001060426
42446CB00040B/850